IN SEARCH OF HONOR

IN SEARCH OF HONOR

By
RONALD A. WILSON

Trafford Publishing
Indiana

Order this book online at www.trafford.com
or email orders@trafford.com

Most Trafford titles are also available at major online book retailers.

Note for Librarians: A cataloguing record for this book is available from Library
and Archives Canada at www.collectionscanada.ca/amicus/index-e.html

Printed in Victoria, BC, Canada.

ISBN: 978-1-4269-0414-1 (sc)
ISBN: 978-1-4269-0415-8 (hc)
ISBN: 978-1-4269-0416-5 (eBook)

Library of Congress Control Number: 2009935555

*Our mission is to efficiently provide the world's finest, most
comprehensive book publishing service, enabling every author to
experience success. To find out how to publish your book, your way, and
have it available worldwide, visit us online at www.trafford.com*

Trafford rev.08/11/09

 www.trafford.com

North America & international
toll-free: 1 888 232 4444 (USA & Canada)
phone: 250 383 6864 ♦ fax: 812 355 4082

For my wise and loving parents, Charles and Jean
Wilson, my daughter Xaun, my son Charles and my
wife Monica.

The Bridge Builder
By
Will Allen Dromgoole

An old man, going a lone highway,
Came at the evening cold and gray,
To a chasm, vast, and deep, and wide,
Through which was flowing a sullen tide.

The old man crossed in the twilight dim;
The sullen stream had no fears for him;
But he turned when safe on the other side,
And built a bridge to span the tide.

"Old man", said a fellow pilgrim near,
"You are wasting strength with building here;
Your journey will end with the ending day;
You never again must pass this way;
You've crossed the chasm, deep and wide-
Why build you the bridge at the eventide?"

The builder lifted his old gray head:
"Good friend in the path I have come, "he said",
"There followeth after me today,
A youth, whose feet must pass this way.

This chasm, that has been naught to me,
To that fair-haired youth may a pitfall be.
He, too, must cross in the twilight dim;
Good friend, I am building the bridge for him."

ACKNOWLEDGMENTS

Charles Wilson Sr. and Charles Wilson Jr.; my father and my older brother. Without their love, I would not have lived past my twenty first birthday.

Attorney Arthur Serota, my mentor and friend and all of the young men who have graduated from The Learning Tree Of Western Massachusetts.

The men of Omega Psi Phi Fraternity Incorporated, especially the brothers of Kappa Chapter at Syracuse University, including but not limited to Keith Johnson, David Archibald, James Thomas and Kenyatta Bell. "Friendship is essential to the soul".

Professor David Hall at Northeastern University School of Law who was instrumental in ensuring that I graduate from law school.

Master Heg Robinson at the Roxbury Tai Chi Academy who taught me the importance of meditation and focus.

Pastor Elwood McDowell who continues to serve as a mentor and a friend.

The Sovereign Military Order of The Temple of Jerusalem, especially my sponsors Chev. Dr. John Black and Chvse. Carol Black. "Non nobis Domine non nobis sed Nomini Tuo da gloriam".

INTRODUCTION

Throughout my teen years and young adulthood, my father would share with me short stories, metaphors, and quotes about the importance of integrity. He also encouraged me to seek individuals and organizations that could help me understand what it meant to be a man.

ONE

God is everlasting to everlasting.
God lives within you.
Work hard to achieve spiritual enlightenment.

The soul is your moral compass.
Your soul is what connects you to God and all of
creation.

TWO

All of us originate from the same life force.
Consequently, we are all spiritually connected.
What affects one can affect all.
Respect nature and preserve it for future generations.

Develop a strong relationship with God.
Many good people have lost their way because they did
not remain focused on God.

THREE

The source of all life is within you.
Tap into the spirit that is a part of you.

Strive to understand the mysteries of life.
Releasing the spirit in you requires time, patience, work,
and dedication.
Ask God to guide you.

FOUR

Self-awareness leads to illumination.
Since we have freewill, God will let us make decisions
and choices even if they are destructive.
In order to strengthen your spirit, you must be
disciplined mentally, and physically.

Strengthen God's presence by strengthening your soul.
If you dedicate a few minutes a day to the study of any
discipline, you will soon become an expert.
The further you stray from God's grace, the easier it is
to do harm and commit evil acts.

FIVE

Submit to God and understand your place in the world.
Our physical lives are temporary.
Our soul is everlasting.
Live to glorify the Lord.

Acknowledge God's authority and submit to his will.
You must not take his authority lightly.
Respect and revere God's holy name.

SIX

Seek God's grace and mercy.
Although you may transgress, God is merciful and compassionate.
God does not want to see you suffer or cause you pain.

If you are sincere when you ask for forgiveness, he will grant it.
Glorify God by treating others with dignity and respect.
Do not use excuses to justify oppressing others.
Be compassionate toward those who suffer.

SEVEN

Your actions should glorify and please God.
Help the less fortunate whenever you have an
opportunity.
Actions do speak louder than words.

God wants you to be happy and healthy.
Avoid people and things that will cause you to sin.
Master and control urges and temptations.

EIGHT

Love must be present in your life in order for your actions to matter.
You are God's child and he loves you.
God's hope is for you to use the gift of life as an opportunity to grow in him and experience his love.

Seek God's light when you feel confused or weak.
God's love is warm and comforting.
It brings peace and solace to a tumultuous existence.
Without knowing God's love, the world is cold and empty.

NINE

Life's journey should be a rewarding one.
Rewards do not come in the form of material gains.
In addition to the positive people and forces that you
will encounter, there will also be negative people and
forces.

Anything worth having is obtainable if you work hard
for it.
Do not seek pleasure over principle.
When hate fills your heart it destroys you.
Do not let anger or hate distort your judgment.
Do not harm others because they are different.

TEN

Do not use religion, politics, ethnicity, or gender as justifications for hateful thoughts and actions.
It is difficult for others to manipulate you when you have a strong connection with God.
Learn how to communicate with God on a constant basis.

Learn to pray and mediate between every breath, and every word.
Protect the weak.
Take time every day to consider the things that are important to you.
Do not prioritize the insignificant.
The things that are important to you must be important to God.

ELEVEN

Esteem truth and seek wisdom in all aspects of your life.
Be honest and learn the importance of integrity.
Honor is balance and harmony with God.

Honesty is more important than loyalty.
Those who are honest and truthful will find favor, forgiveness, and mercy.

TWELVE

Truthful people embody integrity, morality, and justice. Loyalty has its place; however, it very rarely supersedes honesty.

If God is your master, you shall never have to fear the truth or the consequences of being honest.
Do not associate with people or organizations where the cost of loyalty is lies.
There is a difference between knowing what is right and doing what is right.

THIRTEEN

Your mind is the most powerful thing in the universe.
You cannot understand the mysteries of life by hoping
or wishing for answers.
You must study and practice the techniques that will
enhance your ability to understand life's mysteries.

Spend time every day working on the ability to focus
and concentrate.
The ability to focus is a skill that must be developed.
Practice exercises that enhance your ability to think
clearly.
Focus reduces the likelihood of distractions interfering
with your ability to think clearly.

FOURTEEN

Focus improves your reasoning ability.
Determination and perseverance are two attributes
associated with focus.
Focus reveals areas in your life that can be improved.

Learn ways to meditate and focus.
Your environment often distracts you.
Devote the time and thought necessary to make sound
decisions.

FIFTEEN

Prayer and meditation are fundamental aspects of a
healthy life.
They help you control your desires.
Prayer and meditation helps provide balance and reason
in your life.

Prayer and mediation allows you to put aside
selfishness in order to focus on connecting with God.
Prayer and meditation helps you put your life in proper
perspective.

SIXTEEN

Dedication to study, meditation, and prayer helps you comprehend the mysteries of life.
In order for you to understand your purpose, you must study, meditate, and pray.

Prayer and meditation is an effective method of calming your mind and your soul.
When your mind is calm, your body is at rest and your soul is at peace.
Meditation helps your body repair itself.
Meditation reduces stress.

SEVENTEEN

When you do not evaluate situations from different perspectives, you react.
You make choices without considering the long-term impact.

You seek immediate gratification of your senses without appreciating the possible long-term impact on your body, mind, or soul.

EIGHTEEN

Develop your entire self.
Strengthen all aspects of your being.
Balance is a prerequisite to an exceptional life.

Balance makes your achievements more substantial.
You cannot excel in one area of your life, and be
deficient in all others.
Work hard to become a well-rounded person.

NINETEEN

Opportunities are fleeting.
Opportunities often come unannounced and disappear
as quickly as they arrived.

An opportunity often comes disguised as an obstacle.
An obstacle can be a problem or a solution.
Be prepared, you never know when an opportunity will
present itself.

TWENTY

Make choices that take advantage of opportunities.
Every choice has a consequence.
Do not be frightened of failure.
Do not get discouraged.

Obstacles and adversities motivate successful people.
Successful people make the best out of any situation.
Do not become a vulgar careerist.

TWENTY-ONE

Although you may not achieve a short-term goal, you may still achieve your long-term goal.
There are several examples of people who fail to achieve a goal but in the process, they discover something new or wonderful.

As one opportunity disappears another may appear.
Even if you do not achieve a goal, do not stop trying.
Risks allow you to learn and experience new things.

TWENTY-TWO

Singleness of purpose is the road to victory.
Purpose gives your life meaning.
Purpose helps you endure hardships and heartaches.
It is harder to trick someone who is purpose driven.
Always consider how an opportunity may or may not
relate to your purpose.

Spend time evaluating your life and determining your
purpose.
Purpose helps you build in milestones.
Purpose allows you to learn from your mistakes and
build upon your successes.
It is important that you consistently reaffirm your
purpose.

TWENTY-THREE

When you are motivated, your work ethic is increased.
Be diligent.
Inspiration excites your senses and your awareness is
increased.

Be observant and obedient to the things that are
necessary to help you succeed.
Have a clear commitment to success.
Do not set yourself up for failure.
Build bridges to resources and opportunities.

TWENTY-FOUR

People change, circumstances change and priorities change.
You must be able to change when appropriate.

As you change and mature, your goals may also change.
Things that you cared about as a child may not be important to you as an adult.

TWENTY-FIVE

As you succeed, milestones should become checkpoints in your life.
Reflect, re-evaluate, and respond.
Reward yourself when you reach a milestone.

Accountability requires that you take ownership of your successes and failures.
As you begin to change your attitude and your behavior, your life will illuminate new purpose and meaning.

TWENTY-SIX

Establish fundamental principles and values early in life.
Embrace values that are ethical.
Deal with character and value issues in a way that you can understand.

Strong values will help you make difficult decisions.
Your values can be the problem or the solution.
Without good values, it is easy to be misled.
Do what is right, always.
You are your values, beliefs, and principles.

TWENTY-SEVEN

Exposure to good values at an early age is very important.
Embrace values that are healing.
It is difficult for people to respect you if you do not respect yourself.

Your behavior should exude integrity.
Illumine integrity and do not fear forgiveness.
It is important for you to be dignified in everything that you do.

TWENTY-EIGHT

Integrity, dignity, and morality must be a part of you.
Do not let the allure of fame or fortune place you in a
position that compromises your integrity.

Those with honor are courageous and steadfast when
confronted with hardship and disappointment.
You must live by a code of conduct that is ethical and
pro active.
Stand firm against injustice, intolerance and ignorance.

TWENTY-NINE

Conduct that is inconsistent with a healthy lifestyle is
unacceptable.
Individual responsibility equals accountability.
If you have a positive attitude and posses positive
energy, then positive people will gravitate toward you
and good things will happen.

Oppose bigotry, intolerance, and hatred.
Avoid situations and individuals that can compromise
your integrity.

THIRTY

It is comforting to be around other people who accept your behavior or engage in similar conduct.
Possess the basic skills and resources necessary to succeed in life.

You cannot make healthy choices and good decisions without having the skills to do so.
Pay special attention to those who can decide your future.

THIRTY-ONE

Treat your body with dignity and respect.
A healthy body and mind allows you to think clearer,
stay focused and achieve greatness.
Your spiritual, mental, emotional, and physical health is
your wealth.

Develop good personal habits.
Take advantage of opportunities to fix your problems.
Forgive yourself.
Forgive those who ask for it.
Selfishness, greed, ignorance, and arrogance are often
reasons why individuals and groups jeopardize the
survival of many for the benefit of the few.

THIRTY-TWO

Be kind, forgiving, compassionate, and merciful.
All of us will experience a situation when we need
forgiveness or mercy.

Treat others the way that you want to be treated.
Develop and cultivate your ability to function as a
productive member of society.

THIRTY-THREE

Peace is knowing that your choices are consistent with your purpose.
Use prayer, faith, hope, and knowledge to achieve inner peace.

Your life will be more enjoyable if you make unselfish choices.
The more you are in touch with your soul; the better you are at making choices that do not harm others.

THIRTY FOUR

If you can change a person's mind, then you can change their behavior.
Individual protections do not give you the right to harm others.
It is easy to manipulate those who have low self-esteem.
Your obligation to God is your obligation to yourself.

You must not violate the rights of others as you exercise your own.
Act responsibly as you seek to exercise your rights.
Do not take advantage of the poor, the sick, or the weak.
If you control your impulses then you can control your actions.

THIRTY-FIVE

Use your best judgment in deciding how to solve a
problem.
Use your resources to their fullest ability.
Choose your friends wisely.

Be careful in your association with those who do not
respect boundaries.
Those who do not respect boundaries are not
trustworthy.

THIRTY-SIX

If bad people advise you, your behavior will become
destructive.
Develop your self-esteem.
Choices are predictable when you know a person's
heart.

Your experiences and relationships shape who you are.
Evaluate situations before you act.
Suspicion and distrust can destroy a relationship.
If you have a question, ask.

THIRTY-SEVEN

Respect rules and boundaries.
Rules can take many forms.
Rules can be written or unwritten.
Rules promote the sustainability and expansion of
civilization.

Rules should have their basis in values and principle.
All institutions have rules that they expect their
members to obey.
The most common boundaries are laws, regulations,
and guidelines.

THIRTY-EIGHT

Civilized society depends on people acting orderly.
We cannot exist as a civilization or a society without
rules.
Disagreement on the particulars of a rule, do not justify
lawlessness.

When you follow rules that promote integrity, honor,
and morality, it is reflected in the choices that you make
and the life that you live.
In addition to the rules set forth by those that govern,
you must also establish your own personal boundaries.

THIRTY-NINE

Rules help you achieve your goals and live in peace with others.
Before countries there were Natural Laws.
Before governments their were Natural Rights.

Those who make the laws must be accountable to the people.
Those who enforce the law must not let their pride lead to abuse.
Communities have the responsibility of protecting the rights of the citizen and ensuring that power is not being abused or misused.

FORTY

If a law is unjust, it must be abolished.
Laws should maintain order and preserve peace.
Without laws, it is impossible to maintain order.

Laws should help society establish boundaries so that
we can all enjoy progress without infringing on the
rights of others.

FORTY-ONE

Demand accountability from institutions that impact your community.
Demand accountability from organizations that have the greatest influence on your community.

People must know the behavior that is expected of them.

FORTY-TWO

Intelligence, compassion, integrity, and culture are examples of some areas in your life, if developed, which can ensure achievement.
Achieve skills that will make you an asset not a liability.
Do not seek compliments or recognition for your achievements.

Measure and mark your achievements.
Document and keep track of your accomplishments.
Do not underestimate the importance of using your achievements as stepping-stones.
Evaluate the impact that your achievements have on your life.

FORTY-THREE

Outcomes are the results that you hoped to obtain.
Compare and evaluate where you are and where you
were.
Fix what does not work and improve upon or replicate
what does work.

Acknowledge your progress.
Before you begin a task, decide what you want to
achieve and dedicate the appropriate time and resources
toward achieving it.
Always have a clear and realistic understanding of what
you are trying to accomplish.

FORTY-FOUR

Hard work and dedication is very important.
Regardless of the outcome, hard work is its own reward.
A good work ethic usually ensures success.
Work smart.

Dedication is commitment to a task.
Commitment is more than verbal.
Commitment often requires a change in lifestyle.
Although there may be a difficult transition period, if you are dedicated, circumstances will always improve.

FORTY-FIVE

Set objectives regularly.
Objectives reinforce your lifestyle.
They keep you on the correct path toward your goals.
They help you see how far you have come and how far you have to go.

Once an objective is accomplished, reflect on what it took to achieve it.
Keep your objectives obtainable.
If your objective is not obtainable, you will abandon it.

FORTY-SIX

Review and update your objectives to make sure that they are consistent with your goals.
You must have control over your objectives.
Objectives that are beyond your control will destroy your motivation.

Accept ownership of your successes or failures.
If others set your goals, you are living a life that they chose, not you.

FORTY-SEVEN

Have a plan for every significant task.
Always have more than one plan to achieve the same goal.
When you have several plans it is important to put them in proper order.

Your plans should never be written in stone.
Express your plans in a positive manner.
Plans that are healthy and obtainable will help you persevere for the long term.
Planning prevents you from making the same mistakes twice.

FORTY-EIGHT

Planning helps you focus your goals.
Planning forces you to recognize your abilities.
Planning gives you motivation to succeed.

Planning helps you maintain strong forward
momentum.
Plans should reflect the life that you want to live.
Not every plan needs to be an elaborate scheme.

FORTY-NINE

Proper organization will show you the most effective way to achieve your goals.
Manage people and situations by organizing properly.
Organization allows you to weigh costs and benefits of a goal.
Organization helps you use and manage your time effectively.

Organization helps you avoid wasting time and resources.
Organization helps you identify what is important.
Organized people get results.

FIFTY

Goals help you determine where you want to go in life and how you will get there.
Set goals with the intention of them moving you forward in life.

Use common sense when setting a goal.
Goals must be realistic and consistent with your resources and skills.
Daily goals will help you achieve your lifetime goal.

FIFTY-ONE

Set goals slightly out of reach.
Goals that are not challenging will not motivate you.
Concrete goals help you keep obstacles in perspective.
Goals help guide your choices.

Make sure that your goals are intentional.
Precise goals are measurable.
Your goals must have a purpose.
Know your purpose.

FIFTY-TWO

Lifetime goals improve your focus, and determination.
Lifetime goals help you avoid negative influences.

The most wonderful thing about setting a lifetime goal
is the journey that you take to reach it.
You must be a living example of the goals you want to
achieve.

FIFTY-THREE

It is easier to pick short-term goals when you know your lifetime goals.
Short term-goals should help lead toward the accomplishment of your lifetime goals.
Short-term goals should be realistic, challenging, and accomplished quickly.

As your life changes, it is natural for your goals to change.
Be prepared to modify or change all of your goals at a future date.

FIFTY-FOUR

Changes should reflect your growth.
It is easier to keep control over the achievement of
your goals when you own them.
Every great accomplishment requires sacrifice.

Talk about your goals to others.
Have sharp, focused goals.
If you fail to achieve a goal, evaluate the plan that you
had and the obstacles you faced.

FIFTY-FIVE

It is not necessary for you to write all of your goals down.
Do not set goals because of fear.

Make sure that your goals will make you happy.
Assign priority to your goals and review them often.
Use obstacles as stepping-stones and teaching moments.
Work toward accomplishing goals one step at a time.

FIFTY-SIX

Effective leaders inspire others.
A strong community does not need a weak leader.
Strong leaders must work hard to organize a weak community.
Be a decision-maker that the community can rely on.

Strong leaders must make difficult decisions.
As you acquire new skills, transition to the next stage of leadership.
Be transparent.

FIFTY-SEVEN

Do not be deceptive.
Do not exploit others for your own personal gain.
Do not be embarrassed to ask for help.

Do not make your self-look good at someone else's
expense.
Do not make others suffer for your benefit.
Do not ignore good advice.

FIFTY-EIGHT

Learn from your mistakes and the mistakes of others.
Offer suggestions instead of telling people what to do.
Evaluate a situation first, then decide which solutions
are best.

Do not polarize people when trying to solve a problem.
Secure resources before embarking on a project.
Establish boundaries.

FIFTY-NINE

It is always important that you consider the advice of others.
Seek the wisdom and counsel of experts.
Seek the wisdom of mentors who have what you want.
Seek the wisdom and strength of godly men and women.

Open your heart to those who suffer.
Go outside of yourself and out of your way to help make someone else's life better.
Manage your emotions.
Sometime the best approach is an indirect one.
Every decision should be strategic.

SIXTY

When you are arrogant, stubborn, and impulsive, you are easy to manipulate.
Do not demand excellence from someone not capable of it.
Respect the privacy of others.
Use discretion when in public.

Never make a major decision without their being some benefit bestowed on you.
Constantly inventory all of your resources.
Use intelligence to defeat your enemies.
Do not run from your past.

SIXTY-ONE

Master the ability to communicate.
Understand that words trigger emotions.
Communicate with words that are not offensive or
insulting.

Your body language should always be positive.
Always make eye contact when talking to someone.
Conversations have solved more problems than wars.

SIXTY-TWO

Listen, learn, then respond.
Allow people to express themselves before forming a
response.
Respond after someone has finished his or her
thoughts.

Know your audience.
Know yourself.
Your audience should understand what you are saying.
Avoiding a subject or a situation will not make it go
away.

SIXTY-THREE

Knowledge puts you in a position to control your environment.
Knowledge increases your self-esteem and desire to succeed.
Knowledge is liberating and empowering.
Education creates opportunities.

Read and study everyday.
Learn the art of thinking clearly and critically.
The easiest way to obtain knowledge is to stay in school.
Never stop learning.
Distance yourself from people or institutions that are unwilling to share information with you.

SIXTY-FOUR

Ignorance is not an option.
Ignorance prevents you from making informed decisions.
Ignorant people use obstacles as a reason to fail.
Intelligent people use obstacles as an opportunity to move forward.

Everyone can learn something.
The more knowledge that you obtain, the more likely you are to succeed.
Information is power.

SIXTY-FIVE

There is always a place for discretion.
When you are ignorant, you cannot make informed decisions.
Education is a life long adventure.
Education is not selling out.

People are afraid to learn new things when they are uncomfortable with change.
Illiteracy limits ones ability to grow.
Illiterate people cannot be self-sufficient.
Literate people can achieve anything that they desire.

SIXTY-SIX

History can teach great lessons, provide inspiration, and give you goals.
Use history to move you forward.
History teaches you the truth about who you are.
Learn everything that you can about your culture.

Study the strengths and weaknesses of your culture.
Embrace values that celebrate life.
Respect the culture, religion, and ethnicity of others.

SIXTY-SEVEN

Learn about your family ancestry, lineage, and
traditions.
Know your history and embrace your culture.
Do not place your culture above others.

Embrace diversity and learn as much about other
cultures as possible.
Treat all ethnicities with dignity and respect.
People may not remember what you said or what you
did, but they will remember how you treated them.
Healthy relationships are founded on mutual respect.
Everything that has a beginning has an end.

ABOUT THE AUTHOR

Judge Wilson earned his Bachelor of Arts degree from Syracuse University in 1992, and his Jurist Doctorate from Northeastern University School of Law in 1995. After earning his Jurist Doctorate, he was selected as the recipient of the Otto Snowden Community Fellowship from the Urban Law and Public Policy Institute. This institute is a trailblazing program in Boston committed to developing solutions to the challenges facing our nation's inner city communities.

From 1999 to 2002, Ron served as Crime Prevention Specialist for the Pima County Attorney and in March of 2002; he was appointed the Presiding Judge for the City of South Tucson. Judge Wilson's appointment was historically significant. At the age of 33, he became the first full-time Judge for the City of South Tucson, the first African American Presiding Judge in Pima County and one of the youngest Presiding Judges in United States history. Judge Wilson has also instructed courses at the University of Arizona on topics such as Slavery, Jim Crow, the Civil Rights Movement, Black Politics, Black History, and Mentoring At-Risk Youth. He is the recipient of numerous awards and certificates including the Martin Luther King Jr. Drum Major Award, The Rosa Parks Living History Makers Award and The Asa Philip Randolph Social Justice Award. Judge Wilson is the product of the Massachusetts foster care system. He is a transracial adoptee with over 20 adopted siblings. In addition, he has had over 400 foster brothers and sisters.